SANDWICH
FILLINGS

60 easy recipes
for making good food fast

CHANCELLOR
PRESS

First published in Great Britain by Hamlyn
This edition published in 1996 by Chancellor Press
an imprint of Reed Consumer Books Limited,
Michelin House, 81 Fulham Road, London SW3 6RB

ISBN 1 85153 005 3

A CIP catalogue record for this book
is available from the British Library

ACKNOWLEDGEMENTS
Designed and produced by: The Bridgewater Book Company
Series Editors: Veronica Sperling and Christine McFadden
Art Director: Peter Bridgewater
Designer: Terry Jeavons
Photography: Trevor Wood
Food preparation and styling: Jonathan Higgins
Cookery contributor: Christine France

Produced by Mandarin Offset
Printed and bound in Singapore

NOTES

❦ Standard level spoon measurements are used in all recipes.

❦ Both imperial and metric measurements have been given in all
recipes. Use one set of measurements only and not a mixture of both.

❦ Eggs should be size 3 unless otherwise stated.

❦ Milk should be full fat unless otherwise stated.

❦ Fresh herbs should be used unless otherwise stated. If unavailable use
dried herbs as an alternative but halve the quantites stated.

❦ Ovens should be preheated to the specified temperature - if using a
fan assisted oven, follow manufacturer's instructions for adjusting the
time and the temperature.

❦ All microwave information is based on a 650 watt oven. Follow
manufacturer's instructions for an oven with a different wattage.

Contents

Introduction

$\mathcal{T}$HE sandwich is thought to have been invented in 1762 by an Englishman named John Montague, Earl of Sandwich. He spent much of his time gambling, and is reputed to have asked a servant to bring him some meat between slices of bread so that he could eat without having to leave the gaming table.

Sandwiches have certainly moved on since then, and these days there is a sandwich to suit every taste and almost any occasion. They may be hot or cold, savoury or sweet, and with the increasing variety of different breads now available, there is no need to run out of ideas.

Successful Sandwich Making

Always spread butter and/or filling right over the bread, otherwise the edges will be dry. Softened butter is easiest to spread evenly. If you are preparing a lot of sandwiches, a small, flexible palette knife will make spreading much easier.

Try cutting sandwiches in different shapes, using a sharp knife to cut triangles or rectangles, or biscuit cutters for more unusual shapes, such as flowers and animals.

To make sandwiches in advance without them going soggy, use toast or crisp-crusted bread and spread with butter, margarine or cream cheese as a waterproof barrier against moist toppings and fillings. Instead of wet salad ingredients, go for crisp vegetables, such as celery, cabbage or Chinese leaves. Cover with cling film or foil to prevent drying out, then store in a refrigerator or cool place for up to 24 hours.

Packed Lunches

Wrap prepared sandwiches in greaseproof paper, cling film or kitchen foil and pack into polythene boxes or lunchboxes to prevent squashing.

Picnics

To avoid limp, soggy sandwiches on picnics, choose and make sandwiches carefully. Alternatively, take along a selection of different fillings in polythene boxes with various breads and rolls to make sandwiches on the spot. If it is likely that they will have to remain in a warm car for some time, it is worth packing them into a cool bag to keep perishable fillings fresh.

Freezing

Many sandwiches freeze successfully, but certain fillings are unsuitable. Beware of fillings with a high water content – particularly salad ingredients, such as tomatoes and cucumber – which will make the sandwiches too soggy. Hard-boiled egg should also be avoided, as it tends to go rubbery.

Sandwiches can be frozen for up to two months, and take approximately one hour to thaw at room temperature.

Flavoured Butters for Spreading

Use savoury butters to add flavour and variety to meat fillings. Mash softened butter or cream cheese with chopped fresh herbs, garlic, mustard or horseradish to taste.

Danish Open Sandwiches

Serving open sandwiches is an easy way to entertain, as they can be prepared in advance to eliminate any last minute panics. Even easier, you can simply present your guests with a selection of cold meats, cheese, vegetables and garnishes so they can make up their own.

The base of open sandwiches needs to be of firm bread, such as pumpernickel, rye or crispbread. A spreading of butter, topped with a lettuce leaf, prevents the bread absorbing moisture from the topping and becoming soggy. Keep toppings simple and identifiable, and try to include a combination of colours, textures and flavours.

CLOCKWISE FROM THE LEFT: *baguette, bagels, poppy seed roll, pitta bread, wholemeal bread, croissants, ciabatta, rye bread, crusty white sandwich bread.* CENTRE: *cracked wheat rolls, wholemeal roll.*

Reuben's Rye

MAKES 2

6 slices rye or pumpernickel bread
4 tbsp Thousand Island dressing
4 thin slices corned beef

4 thin slices gruyère cheese
5 tbsp sauerkraut
salt and freshly ground black pepper

*S*PREAD 4 bread slices with the dressing. Top each with a slice of corned beef, a slice of gruyère cheese and a generous spoonful of sauerkraut.

❦ Season well, and place 1 covered slice on top of another one.

❦ Top with the remaining bread slices, pressing down firmly, to make triple deckers.

Tandoori Chicken

MAKES 4

100 g/4 oz boned tandoori chicken,
   cut into bite-sized pieces
4 tbsp mayonnaise
1 tsp mild curry powder
1 tbsp seedless raisins
4 rashers back bacon, rinded
8 slices brown bread, crusts removed
   and toasted

4 slices white bread, crusts removed
   and toasted
50 g/2 oz butter
4 lettuce leaves
about 16 thin cucumber slices
1 small green pepper, seeded and
   sliced
2 tomatoes, thinly sliced
1 tbsp chopped fresh parsley

*M*IX the tandoori chicken with the mayonnaise, curry powder and raisins, blending well.

❦ Place the bacon under a preheated hot grill and cook until crisp. Drain on absorbent paper.

❦ Spread 1 side of the brown bread and both sides of the white bread with the butter. Spread the chicken mixture equally over 4 slices of the brown bread. Top each with a slice of white bread. Cover each white slice of bread with a lettuce leaf, 4 of the cucumber slices and slices of green pepper.

❦ Top each sandwich with a final slice of brown bread. Cover with tomato slices and a rasher of bacon. Sprinkle with chopped parsley and serve.

Peppered Mackerel with Avocado

MAKES 2

1 small ripe avocado pear
1 tbsp mayonnaise
1 tbsp lemon juice

4 slices multi-grain bread
1 large fillet peppered smoked
    mackerel, flaked
lemon wedges, to serve

*P*EEL and stone the avocado, and mash the flesh with the mayonnaise and half the lemon juice. Spread the avocado mixture evenly over the bread slices.

❧ Arrange the flaked mackerel on 2 of the slices.

❧ Sprinkle with the remaining lemon juice, and top with the remaining bread slices. Serve with lemon wedges.

Avocado and Prawn Mayonnaise

MAKES 4

8 slices granary bread
50 g/2 oz softened butter
1 ripe avocado pear, halved and
    stoned
juice of 1 lemon

salt and freshly ground black pepper
175 g/6 oz peeled cooked prawns
4 tbsp mayonnaise
cayenne pepper
lettuce leaves

*S*PREAD the bread slices with the butter. Cut the avocado flesh into thin slices and toss in the lemon juice with salt and pepper to taste.

❧ Mix the peeled prawns with the mayonnaise, a little cayenne pepper and salt to taste.

❧ Arrange the avocado slices, prawns and a little lettuce on 4 of the slices, and top with the remaining bread slices.

Aubergine and Pepper Layer

MAKES 4

1 large aubergine
4 tbsp olive oil
1 large red pepper, halved and seeded
1 small ciabatta loaf, thinly sliced

50 g/2 oz red pesto sauce
2 tbsp fresh basil leaves
freshly ground black pepper
basil sprigs, to garnish

*C*UT the aubergine into slices about 1 cm/½ inch thick, and brush with olive oil. Cook under a preheated hot grill for 6-8 minutes, turning once, until soft and golden. Cool.
❧ Cut each pepper half into 4 strips and place under the grill, skin side up, for about 5 minutes or until the skin has blackened and the flesh is soft. Cool, then peel off the skin.
❧ Spread the bread thinly with the pesto sauce. Arrange aubergine slices over one-third of the slices, and some of the pepper strips over another third. Stack the slices in pairs, with basil leaves and pepper between, then top with a third slice, pesto side down.
❧ Press down lightly and garnish with basil sprigs.

Curried Prawn and Coriander

MAKES 4

1 small baguette
2 tsp mild curry paste
75 ml/3 fl oz mayonnaise
2 tbsp chopped fresh coriander

200 g/7 oz peeled cooked prawns
2 spring onions, chopped
salt and freshly ground black pepper
1 tbsp lime or lemon juice

*S*LICE the bread diagonally into fairly thin slices. Mix the curry paste into the mayonnaise.
❧ Stir in the coriander, prawns and onions, and season with salt and pepper to taste.
❧ Spread the mixture over half the bread slices, sprinkle with lime juice and sandwich together.

Malted Banana and Marmalade

MAKES 4

8 slices malt loaf
75 g/3 oz cream cheese

1 large banana, thinly sliced
2 tbsp chunky marmalade

*S*PREAD the slices of malt loaf evenly with the cream cheese. Mix the banana with the marmalade.

❦ Spread the banana and marmalade mixture over 4 of the slices of malt loaf and top with the remaining 4.

❦ Press down lightly, and cut the sandwiches diagonally to make triangles, if liked.

Date, Lemon and Coconut Scones

MAKES 4

4 fresh sweet scones
25 g/1 oz butter or margarine
50 g/2 oz fresh or dried dates,
  pitted and chopped

5 tbsp lemon curd
1 tbsp desiccated coconut, toasted

*S*PLIT the scones across the middle, and spread each half with butter or margarine.

❦ Stir the dates into 4 tbsp of the lemon curd and mix well. Divide the mixture equally between the bottom halves of the scones, and replace the tops.

❦ Brush a little of the remaining lemon curd over the tops of the scones and sprinkle with desiccated coconut.

Club Special

MAKES 2

4 slices each brown and white bread,
  lightly toasted
15 g/½ oz butter per sandwich
salt and freshly ground black pepper
SUGGESTED FILLINGS:
slices of roast beef and lettuce
slices of salami and watercress

prawn mayonnaise
chopped cooked chicken and chopped
  tomato
slices of cooked ham and fruit
  chutney
radishes and parsley sprigs, to
  garnish

*T*HIS is a layered sandwich with a different filling between each layer. Select fillings from the suggestions above and make 2 sandwiches of 3 layers. Butter the toast and cut in half diagonally.

❦ Build up the sandwich layers using alternate triangles of brown and white toast with the selected fillings in between. Season each filling with salt and pepper to taste. Decorate the top toast layer with a radish and a parsley sprig.

BLT (Bacon, Lettuce and Tomato)

MAKES 1

2 rashers lean bacon
2 slices wholemeal or granary bread
2 tbsp mayonnaise

2 crisp lettuce leaves, shredded
1 tomato, sliced
freshly ground black pepper

*G*RILL or fry the bacon until golden brown and crisp, turning once.

❦ Spread the bread with mayonnaise and arrange the bacon, lettuce and tomato over 1 slice. Season with black pepper, and top with the remaining bread slice. Serve hot or cold.

Chicken Triangles

MAKES 16

100 g/4 oz cooked chicken, finely
    chopped
1 slice cooked ham, finely chopped
pinch of paprika
75 g/3 oz butter

2 tbsp mayonnaise
1 tsp finely chopped fresh mint
salt and freshly ground black pepper
8 slices granary bread, crusts
    removed

*M*IX together the chicken, ham and paprika. Beat in
50 g/2 oz of the butter, then add the mayonnaise, mint,
and salt and pepper to taste.

❧ Lightly butter the bread. Spread the chicken filling evenly
over half the slices of bread and top with the other slices. Cut
into triangles and serve.

VARIATION: substitute plain yogurt for the mayonnaise.

Chicken and Almond Roundels

MAKES 8

8 large slices white bread, from a
    sliced loaf
8 large slices brown bread, from a
    sliced loaf
softened butter, for spreading
175 g/6 oz cooked boned chicken,
    finely chopped

2 tbsp soured cream
25 g/1 oz blanched almonds, toasted
    and chopped
salt and freshly ground black pepper
1-2 tbsp redcurrant jelly

*C*UT a round from each slice of bread, using a large fluted
pastry cutter, 9 cm/3½ inches in diameter. Using an apple
corer, cut a 2 cm/¾ inch hole in the centre of each white circle
of bread, leaving a ring.

❧ Spread the circles of brown bread with butter.

❧ Mix the chopped chicken with the soured cream, almonds
and salt and pepper to taste. Spread the brown circles of bread
with the chicken mixture and sandwich together with the rings
of white bread. Spoon a little redcurrant jelly into the 'hole' in
the top of each sandwich.

Beef and Coleslaw

MAKES 1

3 slices hot toast
15 g/½ oz butter
10-12 thin slices cucumber
2 tbsp coleslaw

1 tsp creamed horseradish
2 slices lean rare roast beef
tomato wedges, to garnish
watercress sprigs, to garnish

*S*PREAD the toast on 1 side only with butter. Top 1 slice of toast with a layer of cucumber and coleslaw. Cover with a second slice of toast spread with horseradish.

❧ Arrange the sliced beef on top of the horseradish, and place the third slice of toast on top, buttered side down.

❧ Cut the sandwich in half diagonally and garnish with tomato and watercress.

Pâté, Chutney and Chive

MAKES 24

75 g/3 oz butter
200 g/7 oz coarse meat pâté
2 tbsp chutney

1 tbsp snipped chives
salt and freshly ground black pepper
12 slices wholemeal bread, crusts
removed

*B*EAT together 50 g/2 oz of the butter and the pâté. Add the chutney, chives and salt and pepper to taste, and mix well together.

❧ Lightly butter the bread, and spread the pâté mixture evenly over half the slices. Top with remaining slices, cut into quarters and serve.

VARIATION: substitute mustard butter for plain butter.

Creamy Tuna Specials

MAKES 4

200 g/7 oz can tuna, drained
2 spring onions, chopped
2 crisp lettuce leaves, finely shredded
10 slices cucumber
4 tbsp mayonnaise

3 tbsp tomato ketchup
4 crisp round rolls
40 g/1½ oz butter
4 slices tomato

FLAKE the tuna, and mix in the spring onions and lettuce. Chop 6 slices of the cucumber and add to the tuna.

❧ Mix together the mayonnaise and tomato ketchup, and combine thoroughly with the tuna mixture.

❧ Carefully cut off the top third of each roll. Put the tops to one side to use as lids.

❧ Pull the soft bread out from the centre of the rolls. Spread the butter on the insides of the rolls and on the lids.

❧ Spoon the tuna mixture into the hollowed-out rolls. Place a slice of cucumber and a slice tomato on top of each one. Arrange the lids on top.

Stuffed French Bread

MAKES 3

1 large long crusty French stick
25 g/1 oz butter
COLESLAW:
100 g/4 oz white cabbage, grated
25 g/1 oz onion, grated
1 small carrot, grated
1 celery stick, chopped
15 g/½ oz raisins
3 walnuts, coarsely chopped
3–4 tbsp mayonnaise

FILLING:
2 lettuce leaves, shredded
3 slices mortadella, rolled
25 g/1 oz salami, rolled into cornets
50 g/2 oz smoked cheese, sliced
50 g/2 oz blue cheese, sliced
1 hard-boiled egg, sliced
1 large beef tomato, sliced

TO make the coleslaw, thoroughly mix together the cabbage, onion, carrot, celery, raisins and walnuts. Bind together with the mayonnaise.

❧ Split the loaf in half horizontally. Spread the butter thinly on the inside of the loaf.

❧ Spread the coleslaw along the length of the bottom half of the loaf and top with the lettuce, mortadella, salami, smoked cheese, blue cheese, egg and tomato, arranged attractively.

❧ Press the loaf halves firmly together and cut vertically into 3 thick sections to serve.

Middle Eastern Picnic Chicken

SERVES 8

2 tbsp oil
1 tbsp lemon juice
$\frac{1}{2}$ tsp ground turmeric
1.75 kg/3$\frac{1}{2}$ lb chicken
salt and freshly ground black pepper
75 ml/3 fl oz water
2–3 tbsp chopped mixed fresh herbs

grated zest and juice of $\frac{1}{2}$ lemon
50 g/2 oz pistachio nuts, roughly
    chopped
1 large round sesame loaf, about
    23 cm/9 inches
225 g/8 oz chicken liver pâté

*H*EAT the oil with the lemon juice and turmeric in a heavy-based casserole. Brown the chicken, and season with salt and pepper. Reduce the heat, cover and cook gently for 30 minutes. Add the water, turn the chicken over and cook for a further 45 minutes–1 hour, until the juices run clear.

❧ Cool the chicken in the pan. Skim off the fat and reserve the juices. Cut the chicken meat into bite-size pieces.

❧ Combine the chicken pieces with the herbs, lemon rind, juice, nuts and stock from the cooked chicken.

❧ Cut the top off the loaf and scoop out the bread from the base and lid. (Make breadcrumbs and store for future use.)

❧ Spoon half the chicken mixture into the hollow base of the loaf, cover with the chicken liver pâté and fill up with the remaining chicken. Top with the lid and press down gently.

❧ Wrap in cling film and chill for several hours before serving.

❧ Arrange on a board and cut into wedges like a cake to serve.

Greek Salad Picnic Rolls

MAKES 4

4 sesame seed Vienna rolls or picnic
    baguettes
3 tbsp olive oil
1 garlic clove, crushed
4 Cos or other crisp lettuce leaves,
    coarsely shredded

1 beef tomato, sliced
7 cm/3 inch piece cucumber, diced
100 g/4 oz feta cheese, diced
4 pitted black olives, sliced
salt and freshly ground black pepper

*C*UT the rolls in half lengthways. Brush the cut surfaces with the olive oil and spread thinly with garlic. Divide the lettuce between the rolls, and place the tomato slices on top.

❧ Toss together the cucumber, feta cheese and olives, and spoon onto the rolls. Season to taste.

❧ Press the rolls back together firmly, enclosing the filling. Wrap closely in foil to pack.

Raspberry and Ricotta Bagels

MAKES 4

4 fresh bagels
100 g/4 oz ricotta cheese
4 tbsp raspberry conserve

100 g/4 oz fresh or thawed frozen
   raspberries
icing sugar

*S*PLIT the bagels across the middle, and spread both halves with the ricotta cheese. Spoon the raspberry conserve over the bottom halves.

❦ Arrange the raspberries over the conserve and replace the top half of the bagels. Sprinkle lightly with icing sugar and serve.

VARIATION: for Strawberry Mascarpone Bagels, replace the ricotta with mascarpone or cream cheese, and use strawberry conserve instead of raspberry. Thinly slice 100 g/4 oz fresh strawberries to fill the bagels as above. Sprinkle with icing sugar to serve.

Pear and Mincemeat Teacakes

MAKES 4

4 currant teacakes
75 g/3 oz cream cheese
2 ripe dessert pears

4 tbsp rich mincemeat
lemon juice

*S*PLIT the currant teacakes in half, and spread each half with the cream cheese.

❦ Core 1 of the pears, cut into small dice and stir into the mincemeat. Core and thinly slice the remaining pear, and sprinkle with lemon juice to prevent browning.

❦ Place a spoonful of the mincemeat mixture on the bottom half of each bun. Arrange the pear slices on top, and sandwich the buns back together.

Beef, Cheese and Pickle

MAKES 4

4 large, soft, round sesame rolls
50 g/2 oz butter
100 g/4 oz cold roast beef, shredded
4 tbsp mayonnaise
1-2 tsp creamed horseradish
1 tbsp snipped fresh chives
4 lettuce leaves

100 g/4 oz mature Cheddar cheese,
    thinly sliced
1 tomato, thinly sliced
2 tbsp ploughman's or chunky brown
    pickle
1 medium leek, very thinly sliced
1 tbsp grated lemon rind
1 tbsp seedless raisins

$\mathcal{C}$UT 3 horizontal slits in each roll but do not cut right through to the other side. Spread the bread layers evenly with the butter.

❧ Mix the beef with half the mayonnaise, the horseradish and the chives, blending well.

Place a lettuce leaf on the bottom layer of each roll and top with an equal quantity of the beef filling.

❧ Fill the middle layer of the rolls with slices of cheese, topped with slices of tomato and the pickle.

❧ Mix the leek with the lemon rind, remaining mayonnaise and raisins, blending well. Use to fill the top layer of the rolls. Press the top of each roll down lightly before serving.

Emmenthal and Cherry Tomato

MAKES 4

225 g/8 oz Emmenthal cheese
4 crisp rolls
50 g/2 oz butter
8 small lollo rosso or oakleaf lettuce
    leaves

8 cherry tomatoes, sliced
4 tbsp tomato relish
cucumber slices

$\mathcal{C}$UT half the cheese into 4 slices and grate the remainder. Make 2 cuts diagonally almost through each roll. Butter 1 side of each cut.

❧ Put half the lettuce, the tomatoes, pickle and cheese slices into 1 cut. Put the remaining lettuce, the cucumber and grated cheese in the second cut.

Poppy Seed Knots with Red Salad Filling

MAKES 4

4 poppy seed knots
4 tbsp mayonnaise
175 g/6 oz red cabbage, shredded
50 g/2 oz cooked or pickled beetroot, diced

200 g/7 oz can red kidney beans, drained
½ small red onion, thinly sliced
salt and freshly ground black pepper

*C*UT a slice from the top of each poppy seed knot and reserve for a lid. Scoop out the soft insides (these can be used for breadcrumbs).
❦ Mix together the mayonnaise, cabbage, beetroot, kidney beans and onion. Season well with salt and pepper.
❦ Spoon the mixture into the scooped-out rolls, pressing down firmly. Top with the lids.

Asparagus Rolls

MAKES 60

1 large sliced brown loaf, crusts removed
175 g/6 oz butter

350 g/12 oz can asparagus tips, drained

*U*SING a rolling pin, roll the slices of bread until very thin. Butter a slice of bread and arrange asparagus tips along the long edges. Roll up and place, join-side down, on a tray. Repeat for all the slices of bread, packing the rolls tightly together to stop them unrolling. Refrigerate for 1 hour.
❦ When ready to serve, cut each roll into 3, garnish with more asparagus tips and arrange on a serving dish.

VARIATIONS: cover the bread with very thin slices of ham or smoked salmon before adding the asparagus.

Smoked Salmon Special

MAKES 1

1 slice rye bread
butter, for spreading
2 slices smoked salmon

1 egg, lightly scrambled
parsley sprigs, to garnish

*S*PREAD the bread with the butter. Cover the salmon slices with the scrambled egg and roll up. Place on top of the buttered rye bread. Garnish with parsley sprigs.

New Yorkers

MAKES 8

8 slices rye bread
225 g/8 oz cream cheese
4 slices smoked salmon

1 red onion, sliced into rings
16 sprigs fresh coriander
freshly ground black pepper

*S*PREAD the slices of bread thickly with the soft cheese. Cut each slice of smoked salmon in half and roll into a small cornet shape. Place a smoked salmon cornet on top of each slice of bread.
❧ Top with a few rings of red onion and coriander sprigs. Season with pepper and serve.

Smoked Salmon Triangles

MAKES 32

4 slices brown bread, crusts removed
25 g/1 oz butter
100 g/4 oz smoked salmon, very
  thinly sliced

freshly ground black pepper
lemon juice
lemon slices and parsley sprigs, to
  garnish

*S*PREAD the bread with the butter. Cover each slice with smoked salmon and sprinkle with pepper and lemon juice. Cut the slices into 8 triangles, and serve garnished with lemon slices and parsley sprigs.

VARIATIONS: substitute cream cheese, mayonnaise or lemon butter for plain butter. Substitute lime slices, parsley sprigs, sliced stuffed olives or poppy or sesame seeds for lemon slices as garnish.

Pork and Prune

MAKES 20

5 large slices of day-old white bread,
  crusts removed
50 g/2 oz butter
200 g/7 oz cold cooked pork, cut into
  10 slices
100 g/4 oz cottage cheese with chives

salt and freshly ground black pepper
10 no-soak prunes, halved and stoned
10 large orange slices, rind, pith and
  seeds removed
watercress or parsley sprigs,
  to garnish

SPREAD the bread with plenty of butter, and cut each
slice neatly into quarters with a sharp knife.

❦ Cut each slice of pork in half. Place 1 slice of pork on each
piece of bread, and trim to the same size if necessary.

❦ Put 1 heaped teaspoon cottage cheese on each quarter and
season with salt and pepper.

❦ Place a prune half on top of the cottage cheese and press
down firmly.

❦ Cut the orange slices into quarters and arrange 2 quarters on
either side of the prunes to form a 'butterfly'. Garnish with
watercress or parsley sprigs.

Garlic Sausage and Cream Cheese

MAKES 28

7 slices pumpernickel bread
100 g/4 oz cream cheese
salt and freshly ground black pepper

28 thin slices garlic sausage, rinds
  removed
parsley or coriander sprigs, to garnish

CUT the pumpernickel slices into quarters, and spread each
one thickly with the cream cheese. Season with salt and
pepper to taste.

❦ Fold each slice of garlic sausage in half, and cut almost into
two. Twist each half in opposite directions and place on the
cream cheese, pressing down gently.

❦ Garnish with parsley or coriander sprigs, and add more
seasoning if liked.

Fig, Walnut and Dolcelatte

MAKES 4

100 g/4 oz dolcelatte or other soft
   blue cheese
4 small slices firm walnut or rye bread

25 g/1 oz walnut halves
4 ripe figs, sliced or cut into thin
   wedges

*M*ASH the cheese, and spread evenly over the bread. Chop half the walnuts, and sprinkle over the cheese. Arrange the figs over the cheese, and top with the remaining walnut halves.

Chocolate and Apple Toppers

MAKES 4

4 crispbreads
4 tbsp chocolate spread
1 red eating apple

1 green eating apple
juice of ½ lemon
curls of chocolate, to decorate

*S*PREAD the crispbreads evenly with chocolate spread. Core and thinly slice the apples, and toss in the lemon juice to prevent browning. Arrange alternate red and green slices over the chocolate spread. Sprinkle the curls of chocolate over the top and serve.

VARIATION: for Chocolate, Apple and Hazelnut Toppers, substitute chocolate and hazelnut spread for the chocolate spread. Cover the crispbreads with the spread, top with apples as in the main recipe then sprinkle with flaked hazelnuts, either instead of the grated chocolate or in addition to it.

Mackerel Salad

MAKES 24

6 large slices rye or wholemeal bread
40 g/1½ oz butter
2 x 100 g/4 oz cans mackerel fillets in
   tomato sauce, flaked

2 tsp lemon juice
2 tbsp mayonnaise
freshly ground black pepper
4 hard-boiled eggs, sliced, to garnish

*S*PREAD the bread with plenty of butter, and cut neatly into quarters with a sharp knife.

❧ Mix the flaked mackerel with the lemon juice, mayonnaise and pepper to taste, then spread on the buttered bread, dividing the mixture equally among the quarters.

❧ Garnish the top of each quarter with a slice of egg.

VARIATION: substitute canned tuna or sardines in tomato sauce for the mackerel fillets.

Liver Pâté and Cream Cheese

MAKES 1

50 g/2 oz liver pâté
1 crispbread, buttered
1 hard-boiled egg, sliced

25 g/1 oz cream cheese
parsley sprigs, to garnish

*S*PREAD the liver pâté evenly over the crispbread. Top with the hard-boiled egg, spread or pipe on the cheese, and garnish with the parsley sprigs.

Slimmer's Sardine and Cucumber

MAKES 1

1 slice granary bread
1 tsp low-calorie spread
lettuce leaf

8 slices cucumber
75 g/3 oz canned sardines, drained

*L*IGHTLY cover the bread with the low-calorie spread. Arrange the lettuce leaf and cucumber slices on the bread, and top with the sardines.

VARIATION: substitute shrimps for the sardines.

Slimmer's Pear and Ham

MAKES 1

1 slice wholemeal bread
1 tsp low-calorie spread

25 g/1 oz prosciutto or Parma ham
½ ripe pear, peeled, cored and diced

*L*IGHTLY cover the bread with the low-calorie spread. Place the ham in curls on the bread. Pile the pear on top.

Slimmer's Asparagus and Crab

MAKES 1

1 slice rye bread
1 tsp low-calorie spread
4 canned asparagus spears, trimmed

75 g/3 oz crab meat
1 lemon slice, to garnish

*L*IGHTLY cover the bread with the low-calorie spread. Arrange the asparagus spears on half the slice. Flake the crab meat with a fork and spoon onto the other half of the bread. Garnish with the lemon slice.

VARIATION: when fresh asparagus is in season, use in place of the canned asparagus.

Fried Silverside with Pickle

MAKES 4

25 g/1 oz butter
8 large slices white bread
4 tbsp sweet pickle
4 slices cooked beef silverside
2 eggs, beaten

75 ml/3 fl oz milk
freshly ground black pepper
1 tbsp oil
shredded lettuce, to garnish

BUTTER the slices of bread and spread with the pickle. Lay the beef on 4 of the bread slices and cover with the remaining slices. Press gently together, then cut each sandwich in half diagonally to make 2 triangles.

❦ Beat the eggs with the milk and pepper to taste. Dip the sandwiches in the egg mixture to coat well all over.

❦ Heat the oil in a frying pan, add the sandwiches in batches and fry until golden brown on both sides. Serve hot, garnished with shredded lettuce.

Salami and Mozzarella Toasts

MAKES 4

4 thick slices farmhouse crusty bread
100 g/4 oz salami, rinded and thinly
  sliced
4 tomatoes, skinned and sliced
salt and freshly ground black pepper
1 green or yellow pepper, seeded and
  sliced

75 g/3 oz mozzarella cheese, thinly
  sliced
1 tsp dried mixed herbs
4–8 small black olives
sprigs of parsley, to garnish

PLACE the bread under a preheated hot grill and toast until golden on 1 side.

❦ Turn the bread slices over and cover with the salami and tomatoes, adding salt and pepper to taste. Top with the pepper slices and cheese. Sprinkle over the herbs, place under a preheated moderate grill and toast for about 10 minutes until cooked through and bubbling.

❦ Serve hot, topped with the black olives and garnished with sprigs of parsley.

Pigs in Blankets

MAKES 4

4 rashers streaky bacon, rinded
1–2 tsp French mustard
4 frankfurters
2 tbsp vegetable oil

4 long soft rolls
25 g/1 oz butter
75–125 g/3–4 oz coleslaw

*S*PREAD one side of the bacon rashers with a little mustard. Wrap a bacon rasher around each frankfurter, with the mustard on the inside.

❧ Heat the oil in a frying pan. Add the frankfurters, and fry for 10 minutes over a moderately high heat, shaking the pan occasionally, until the bacon is browned on all sides.

❧ Split the rolls in half lengthways, and spread the cut surfaces with butter and a little mustard, if liked. Place 1 frankfurter in each roll, then top with coleslaw.

VARIATIONS: skinless sausages can be substituted for the frankfurters, although they will need to be cooked for an extra 5 minutes.

Any kind of salad can be used instead of coleslaw, or the rolls can be filled with tomato and cucumber slices and lettuce, then dressed with mayonnaise.

Hot Dog Toasties

MAKES 1

1 tbsp oil
1 small onion, cut into thin rings
15 g/1 oz butter
2 large slices white bread

1 frankfurter, cut into rounds
1 tbsp mustard pickle
salt and freshly ground black pepper

*H*EAT the oil in a pan, add the onion rings and fry gently until tender and light golden.

❧ Spread the butter evenly over the bread. Place 1 slice of bread, buttered side down, on the rack of the grill.

❧ Mix the onion rings with the frankfurter, pickle and salt and pepper to taste. Spread the frankfurter and onion mixture evenly over the slice of bread on the rack. Top with the other slice, buttered side uppermost. Press the bread gently together.

❧ Place the sandwich under a preheated moderately hot grill and cook for 4–5 minutes, turning the sandwich once. Serve immediately.

Fishermen's Sticks

MAKES 6

12 fish fingers
melted butter or oil, for brushing
salt and freshly ground black pepper
6 long crusty bread rolls

tomato ketchup
2 small packets potato crisps
3 tomatoes, cut into thin wedges

*B*RUSH the fish fingers with melted butter or oil. Place under a preheated moderately hot grill and cook for 8–10 minutes, turning them once. Add salt and pepper to taste.

❧ Split the rolls lengthways, without cutting them right through. Brush inside each roll with melted butter or oil and put on a baking sheet. Bake in a preheated oven at 190°C/375°F/gas mark 5 for 5 minutes.

❧ Spread the cut surface of the rolls with ketchup. Fill each one with a layer of potato crisps, 2 cooked fish fingers and a few tomato wedges. Serve immediately.

Toasted Tuna and Egg

MAKES 1

2 large slices white bread
15 g/½ oz butter
1 hard-boiled egg, chopped
1 spring onion, trimmed and chopped

1 tbsp flaked tuna
2 tbsp mayonnaise
salt and freshly ground black pepper
parsley sprigs, to garnish

*S*PREAD both slices of bread thinly and evenly with the butter. Place 1 slice of bread, buttered side down, on the rack of the grill.

❧ Mix the hard-boiled egg with the spring onion, tuna, mayonnaise, and salt and pepper to taste. Spread the tuna and egg mixture evenly over the slice of bread on the rack. Top with the other slice, buttered side uppermost. Press the slices of bread gently together.

❧ Place the sandwich under a preheated moderately hot grill and cook for 4–5 minutes, turning the sandwich once. Serve immediately, garnished with parsley sprigs.

Grilled Greek Pitta Pockets

MAKES 4

4 pitta breads
125 g/4 oz cooked lamb, finely
  shredded
1 small bunch spring onions, trimmed
  and chopped
2 lettuce leaves, shredded

2 tomatoes, skinned, seeded and
  chopped
4 black olives, pitted and sliced
2–3 tbsp yogurt salad dressing
salt and freshly ground black pepper
75 g/3 oz feta cheese, crumbled

*C*AREFULLY cut a slit across the top of each pitta bread
but not through to the base. Gently open out the bread to
form pockets.

❧ Mix the lamb with the onions, lettuce, tomatoes, olives,
dressing and salt and pepper to taste, blending well.

❧ Divide the salad mixture equally between the pitta pockets,
and place on a grill rack. Sprinkle over the cheese.

❧ Place under a preheated moderate grill and cook for about
5–6 minutes until golden and bubbly. Serve at once, whole or
cut through into halves.

Pitta and Salami Specials

MAKES 4

4 pitta breads
heart of 1 Cos lettuce, shredded
1 medium onion, coarsely chopped
2 tsp olive oil
175 g/6 oz feta or mozzarella cheese,
  diced

100 g/4 oz salami, thinly sliced
50 g/2 oz pitted black olives, chopped
salt and freshly ground black pepper

*W*RAP the pieces of pitta bread loosely in foil. Place in a
preheated oven at 180°C/350°F/gas mark 4 for about 5
minutes.

❧ Unwrap the bread and make a slit lengthways down 1 side of
each piece to form a pocket.

❧ Place a layer of shredded lettuce and a little onion in each
pocket, and drizzle over a little olive oil.

❧ Divide the cheese, salami and olives equally between the pitta
pockets. Season to taste. Serve immediately while still warm.

Burger Relish Boats

MAKES 4

40 g/1½ oz soft margarine
1 tbsp tomato, sweetcorn or mild chilli relish
2 tsp corn oil
6 fresh or frozen beefburgers

1 large onion, sliced and separated into rings
4 long crusty rolls
8 slices tomato
8 slices cucumber
shredded lettuce, to garnish

*M*IX the margarine and the relish together in a small bowl. Heat the oil in a frying pan, add the beefburgers and cook for 3 minutes, turning once. Add the onion rings and fry for 2 minutes. Transfer the beefburgers and onions to a plate, using a fish slice.

❧ Cut the rolls lengthways along the centre of the tops, cutting almost down to the bottom crust, but do not cut right through.

❧ Open out each roll and spread the margarine and relish mixture inside and over the top. Put all the rolls on a large piece of foil. Cut the beefburgers in half and arrange 3 pieces in each roll. Add a few onion rings to each one.

❧ Wrap the foil around the rolls to cover them completely, and place the foil parcel on a baking sheet. Cook in a preheated oven at 190°C/375°F/gas mark 5 for 10 minutes.

❧ Remove the baking sheet from the oven, and fold back the foil so that the tops of the rolls are uncovered. Return them to the oven for a further 5 minutes to crisp up.

❧ When the tops are crisp, remove from the oven, add the slices of tomato and cucumber to each roll and arrange them on a serving plate, garnished with shredded lettuce.

Toasted Bacon and Mushroom

MAKES 4

25 g/1 oz butter
8 streaky bacon rashers, rinded and chopped
225 g/8 oz mushrooms, sliced

1 tsp dried mixed herbs
salt and freshly ground black pepper
2 eggs, beaten
8 slices buttered bread

*M*ELT the butter in a frying pan, add the bacon and mushrooms and fry until golden. Stir in the herbs and salt and pepper to taste. Pour in the eggs and cook until lightly set. Spread the mixture onto 4 of the bread slices and top with the remaining bread, buttered sides down.

❧ Place the sandwiches on a preheated moderate grill and toast until they are golden brown. Serve immediately.

Fruity Brunch Muffins

MAKES 4

100 g/4 oz no-soak dried fruit salad
  mix, chopped
100 ml/4 fl oz apple juice

4 fruit and spice muffins
50 g/2 oz butter or margarine
30 ml/2 tbsp thick honey

*P*LACE the fruit and apple juice in a small pan, and bring to the boil. Simmer, uncovered, over a moderate heat for 5 minutes, or until no free liquid remains.

❦ Split the muffins and toast on both sides until golden brown.

❦ Mix together the butter and honey, and spread over the muffins. Top each with a spoonful of the fruit, sandwich together again and serve immediately.

Toasted Traffic Lights

MAKES 4

8 slices white or brown bread from a
  sliced loaf, crusts removed
75 g/3 oz cream cheese

1 tbsp strawberry or raspberry jam
1 tbsp apricot jam
1 tbsp greengage jam

*C*UT each slice of bread into a rectangle about 10 x 6.5 cm/4 x 2½ inches.

❦ Toast half the bread slices on 1 side only. Spread the untoasted sides with the cream cheese.

❦ Using a 2.5 cm/1 inch round cutter, stamp out 3 rounds from the remaining slices, then place on top of the cream cheese.

❦ Spoon the strawberry, apricot and greengage jams into the holes, to resemble traffic lights. Toast quickly until lightly browned. Cool slightly before serving.

Spiced Citrus Croissants

MAKES 4

4 large croissants
1 medium orange
4 tbsp fromage frais

1 small ruby or pink grapefruit
1 tsp ground cinnamon

*P*LACE the croissants on a baking sheet and bake in a preheated oven at 200°C/400°F/gas mark 6 for about 5 minutes, until thoroughly heated.

❦ Meanwhile, grate half the zest from the orange and stir into the fromage frais.

❦ Cut all the peel and white pith from the orange and grapefruit, and carefully remove the segments with a sharp knife. Mix with the cinnamon. Heat gently in a small pan for 1–2 minutes.

❦ Split the croissants across the middle and spoon in the fruit mixture. Top with a spoonful of fromage frais, and replace the top halves. Serve immediately.

VARIATION: for Toffee Apple Croissants, core and thickly slice 2 dessert apples and fry in 40 g/1½ oz butter for 1 minute. Add 40 g/1½ oz caster sugar, and stir until caramelized and golden. Spoon into the hot croissants as above, and top each with 1 tablespoon Greek yogurt.

Toasted Turkey and Sweetcorn

MAKES 4

225 g/8 oz cooked turkey meat, diced
2 tbsp mayonnaise
1 celery stick, finely chopped
100 g/4 oz Cheddar cheese, grated

200 g/7 oz can sweetcorn kernels, drained
50 g/2 oz butter
8 slices wholemeal bread

*M*IX together the turkey, mayonnaise, celery, cheese and corn. Butter the bread and divide the turkey mixture evenly between half the slices. Top with the remaining slices, pressing gently together. Melt the remaining butter.

❦ Place the sandwiches on the grill rack and brush with melted butter. Grill under a preheated moderate grill until the bread is browned, then turn over and brush with more melted butter. Continue grilling until the other sides of the sandwiches are browned. Serve hot.

Toasted Garlic Sausage and Cheese Baguette

SERVES 4

1 small baguette
50 g/2 oz butter
1 garlic clove, crushed
8 slices Edam cheese

8 sliced oak-smoked ham
8 slices garlic sausage
1 beef tomato, thinly sliced

*M*AKE 8 regular crosswise cuts along the length of the loaf almost to the base.

❧ Cream the butter with the garlic, and spread between the slices of bread. Place 1 slice of cheese, ham, garlic sausage and tomato in each cut. Press gently together to reshape the loaf.

❧ Cover the loaf loosely with foil, and bake in a preheated oven at 190°C/375°F/gas mark 5 for 10–15 minutes. Remove the top of the foil and cook for a further 5 minutes or until golden. Pull apart or cut between the slices and serve immediately.

Souffléd Ham

MAKES 4

4 small cob rolls
65 g/2½ oz butter
100 g/4 oz ham sausage, sliced
40 g/1½ oz plain flour
200 ml/7 fl oz milk
2 small eggs, separated

50 g/2 oz gruyère cheese, grated
2 tsp chopped fresh mixed herbs
1 small canned pimiento, finely
   chopped
salt and freshly ground black pepper

*C*UT the top off each of the rolls and scoop out the soft bread from inside (use to make breadcrumbs for another dish). Coat the outside of each roll with 25 g/1 oz of the butter.

❧ Wrap the outer crusts in foil but leave the tops exposed. Line the insides of each bread 'nest' with slices of ham sausage.

❧ Melt the remaining butter in a pan. Add the flour and cook for 1 minute, stirring. Gradually add the milk, blending well. Bring to the boil and cook for 2–3 minutes, stirring. Remove from the heat and allow to cool slightly.

❧ Add the egg yolks to the sauce, together with the cheese, herbs, pimiento and seasoning. Whisk the egg whites until they form stiff peaks. Fold into the soufflé mixture.

❧ Divide the soufflé mixture equally between the bread 'nests'. Bake in a preheated oven at 190°C/375°F/gas mark 5 for 25–30 minutes or until well risen and golden. Serve at once.

French Bread Burgers

SERVES 4

1 long French stick
450 g/1 lb sirloin steak, minced
1 tbsp finely chopped onion
2 tbsp grated cheese
1 level tsp salt

½ tsp dried oregano
2 tbsp tomato ketchup or purée
2–3 tomatoes, sliced
extra cheese or anchovy fillets, to
  garnish

$\mathcal{C}$UT the bread into slices, ½–¾ inch thick. Combine the steak, onion, cheese and seasonings. Spread the mixture over the bread slices.

❦ Place under a preheated moderate grill for about 7 minutes until the meat is cooked. Top each with a slice of tomato and cook for a further 2–3 minutes.

❦ Sprinkle a little grated cheese onto each or top with an anchovy fillet. Serve open or sandwiched in pairs, with salad.

Steak and Fried Egg Toast

MAKES 1

oil, for frying
1 thin rump or entrecôte steak, about
  100 g/4 oz
salt and freshly ground black pepper

2 thin slices white bread
1 egg
1 tsp French mustard
watercress, to garnish

$\mathcal{H}$EAT the oil in a frying pan until hot. Add the steak and cook for about 3 minutes on each side (medium done), seasoning to taste. Remove from the pan and set aside.

❦ Heat sufficient oil in the pan to give a depth of about 5 mm/¼ inch. Add the 2 slices of bread, turning them over in the hot oil. Cook steadily until the undersides are golden.

❦ Turn the slices of fried bread over, making room for the egg. Carefully crack the egg into the pan. Fry steadily for 2–3 minutes until the egg is just set. If the bread starts to brown too much, remove it from the pan and keep warm.

❦ Spread 1 slice of fried bread with the mustard. Top with the steak, some of the pan juices, the fried egg, and finally the second slice of fried bread. Garnish with watercress and serve immediately.

Chicken and Ham Loaf

SERVES 6-8

1 crusty sandwich loaf
75 g/3 oz butter
2 small onions, finely chopped
225 g/8 oz mushrooms, thinly sliced
1 tbsp chopped fresh parsley
salt and freshly ground black pepper
225 g/8 oz sausage meat

175 g/6 oz lean bacon, rinded and
    chopped
225 g/8 oz cooked ham, chopped
2 tbsp dry sherry (optional)
½ tsp dried mixed herbs
225 g/8 oz cooked chicken meat,
    skinned, boned and chopped

*C*UT a 1 cm/½ inch slice lengthways off the top of the loaf
and carefully pull out the soft bread inside. Leave a 1
cm/½ inch inner lining of bread to keep the shape. Make
breadcrumbs with the inner bread.
❧ Melt 50 g/2 oz of the butter and brush over the inside and
outside of the loaf. Replace the lid and brush with any
remaining melted butter. Place on a baking sheet and bake in a
preheated oven at 190°C/375°F/gas mark 5 for 10 minutes.
❧ Meanwhile, melt the remaining butter in a pan. Add the
onions, and fry until soft. Add the mushrooms and cook for 2
minutes. Stir in the parsley, season and remove from the heat.
❧ Mix the sausage meat with the bacon, ham and 3 tablespoons
of the breadcrumbs. Stir in the sherry, if using, and the herbs.
❧ Press half the sausage meat mixture into the bread case.
Cover with half the onion mixture. Arrange the chicken on top
and cover with the remaining onion and sausage meat
mixtures. Replace the lid and wrap the loaf in foil.
❧ Return to the oven and bake for 1 hour. Serve the loaf, hot or
cold, cut into thick slices and accompanied with salad.

Pastrami Toasts

MAKES 4

4 tbsp double cream
2 tsp Dijon mustard
175 g/6 oz thinly sliced pastrami, cut
    into thin strips

4 lettuce leaves
4 slices rye bread, toasted and
    buttered
2 large dill pickles, thinly sliced

*H*EAT the cream and mustard over a medium heat until
hot and bubbling. Stir in the pastrami and toss gently
to coat. Heat for a further 1–2 minutes, without boiling.
❧ Place a lettuce leaf on each slice of toast. Cover with a layer
of sliced dill pickle and top with the creamy pastrami mixture.

Croque Monsieur

SERVES 2

50 g/2 oz butter
4 slices bread from a white sandwich loaf
2 slices gruyère cheese

2 thin slices lean cooked ham
freshly ground black pepper
3 tbsp sunflower oil

SPREAD half the butter over 1 side of the bread only. Place a slice of cheese on 2 of the buttered slices, top with a slice of ham and season with a little black pepper. Top with the remaining slice of bread, pressing down firmly.

Melt the remaining butter with the oil in a frying pan, and fry the croques until golden brown, turning once. Serve immediately.

Croque Madame

MAKES 4

125g /4 oz back bacon, rinded and cut in half lengthways
8 thin slices white bread, crusts removed

1–2 tsp wholegrain mustard
125 g/4 oz gruyère cheese, sliced
2 tomatoes, thinly sliced
40 g/1½ oz butter, melted

PLACE the bacon under a preheated hot grill and cook until crisp. Drain on absorbent paper.

Spread half the bread slices with mustard to taste. Top with the cheese, bacon and tomato slices divided equally between them. Cover with the remaining bread, pressing down well.

Place the sandwiches on a baking sheet and brush the tops with half the butter. Bake in a preheated oven at 230°C/450°F/gas mark 8 for about 5 minutes, or until lightly browned.

Using tongs, turn over the sandwiches and brush with the remaining butter. Bake for a further 3–5 minutes. Cut diagonally in half and serve immediately.

Mushroom and Beef Stroganoff Toasts

MAKES 4

450 g/1 lb rare roast beef	5 tbsp soured cream
salt and freshly ground black pepper	pinch of cayenne pepper
25 g/1 oz butter	1 tbsp snipped fresh chives
2 tbsp finely chopped onion	4 slices wholemeal or rye bread
175 g/6 oz button mushrooms, sliced	curly endive or watercress sprigs,
5 tbsp mayonnaise	to garnish

*S*LICE the beef across the grain into fairly thick slices. Shred into fine strips about 5 cm/2 inches long. Season generously with salt and pepper.

❦ Melt the butter in a frying pan. Add the onion and cook for 2 minutes. Add the mushrooms and cook for a further 2 minutes.

❦ Remove from the heat, and stir in the mayonnaise, cream, cayenne pepper and chives.

❦ Place the slices of bread under a preheated hot grill and toast until golden on both sides.

❦ Add the beef to the stroganoff mixture and heat for about 1 minute over a very gentle heat. Do not boil.

❦ Top the slices of toast with curly endive or watercress and spoon over the Stroganoff. Serve at once.

Grilled Peperoni Baguette

MAKES 2

1 tbsp olive oil	1 small baguette
1 small onion, chopped	salt and freshly ground black pepper
1 garlic clove, crushed	50 g/2 oz peperoni sausage, sliced
200 g/7 oz can chopped tomatoes	75 g/3 oz mozzarella cheese, diced
2 tbsp tomato purée	4 pitted black olives, quartered
1 tbsp finely chopped fresh oregano	
or 1 tsp dried oregano	

*H*EAT the oil and gently fry the onion and garlic for 5 minutes, until softened. Add the tomatoes, tomato purée and oregano. Bring to the boil, reduce the heat and simmer until most of the liquid has evaporated.

❦ Slice the baguette in half lengthways. Spread the tomato mixture evenly over the cut surface, and season to taste. Arrange the peperoni slices, mozzarella and olives on top.

❦ Place under a preheated grill for 4–5 minutes, or until golden brown and bubbling. Serve at once.